D1666089

David Burkhart

Stylistic traps in technical English – and how to avoid them

Stilistische Fallen im Technischen Englisch – und wie man sie umgeht

Ein Ratgeber aus der Praxis für die Praxis
2., überarbeitete Auflage

BDÜ Fachverlag

David Burkhart

Stylistic traps in technical English – and how to avoid them

Stilistische Fallen im Technischen Englisch – und wie man sie umgeht

Ein Ratgeber aus der Praxis für die Praxis
2., überarbeitete Auflage

Die Deutsche Bibliothek – CIP Einheitsaufnahme

David Burkhart:
Stylistic traps in technical English – and how to avoid them

Stilistische Fallen im Technischen Englisch – und wie man sie umgeht

Ein Ratgeber aus der Praxis für die Praxis
2., überarbeitete Auflage

ISBN: 978-3-938430-61-3

verlegt von der BDÜ Weiterbildungs- und Fachverlagsgesellschaft mbH, Berlin,
einem Unternehmen des Bundesverbandes der Dolmetscher und Übersetzer e. V. (BDÜ)

© 2007, 2014 · BDÜ Weiterbildungs- und Fachverlagsgesellschaft mbH, Berlin
Satz: Thorsten Weddig, Essen
Foto: Alterfalter/Fotolia.com (Titelbild)
Druck: Schaltungsdienst Lange oHG, Berlin

Introduction

This book is based on the author's professional experience as a technical writer, editor and translator. As an editor for texts written in English by German developers, I soon discovered that the authors tended to make many of the same mistakes. Some of these involved fairly trivial errors, such as using the wrong word (e.g. "actual" for "aktuell"). However, other problems went much deeper, involving issues of style. The fundamental question is always: How can complicated technical matters be expressed adequately in English that is simple, direct and easy to understand? This is not a trivial task, especially when the author's thoughts are expressed in German sentences which are long, complicated and overly abstract.

It occurred to me that German developers could be offered a focused crash course on technical writing in English. Wouldn't that be more efficient – and less expensive – than correcting the same mistakes time and time again?

This book is the result of my work in creating such a course. It has been my privilege to give the course a number of times, as a compact seminar. Based on this experience, the material presented here has evolved – and hopefully improved. Due to time constraints, it is often necessary to cut corners in the seminar and leave some material out. This book provides the full extent of the material.

The objective in all of technical writing is to explain complex topics in simple, direct language. It is the aim of this work to give the reader a toolbox of stylistic techniques, enabling him or her to perform this challenging task in English. Germans will have to reflect on communication styles which are typical of their native language but which may cause problems when applied to English. Ideally, the reader will be able to write like a native speaker of English – a significant professional qualification for many people. Even a casual reader will probably be able to recognize basic stylistic minefields, and can – hopefully – tiptoe around them.

Please note that this is a work on questions of style. In the interest of brevity and focus, it will be assumed throughout that sources of German/English technical terminology are readily available, and that the terminology used here is correct.

Examples are given throughout the book, In order to demonstrate how the stylistic recommendations can be applied. The exercises at the end of each chapter allow the reader to investigate the material in a practical way. The reader is strongly recommended to do these exercises.

The final section of the book provides a suggested solution for each exercise. In many cases comments are added, because the reader's solution could be quite different than mine. Some of these comments also point out various stylistic traps in the exercises which the reader might not have noticed.

The text often uses a German sentence as the starting point. In such cases, the exploration begins with a statement in German, followed by a poor translation and discussion. In other cases, I begin a topic with an example sentence in English which I then analyze. Please note that this varies, without warning.

This book is structured around a number of stylistic "traps", as follows:

Chapter	For German text which …	The trap is …
1	uses German technical jargon	translating directly, literally
2	is substantival	writing substantival English
3	uses long sentences	writing long sentences in English
4	uses the passive voice inappropriately	using the passive voice in English, too
5	makes several statements in one sentence	expressing all of the statements in one long English sentence
6	expresses technical processes in substantival incomplete sentences	translating literally
7	makes a vague statement, when it should be telling people what to do	writing an equally vague statement in English
8	uses nonstandard word order for emphasis	violating the English rules for word order
9	includes words which are not saying anything	translating uncritically
10	uses typographical shortcuts	translating literally
11	makes a general statement, instead of telling people what to do	translating literally
12	uses noun-verb combinations	translating with a noun-verb combination
13	conveys much information before the noun	translating literally

Chapter	For German text which ...	The trap is ...
14	uses complicated verbs	using a complicated verb in English – probably the wrong one
15	does not clearly identify and differentiate cause and effect	translating uncritically
16	deals with practical things in abstract or vague language	translating into abstract, vague English
17	packs too much information into one sentence	expressing all of the information in one English sentence
18	includes commas	violating the English rules for commas
19	includes hyphens	violating the English rules for hyphens

Characteristics of excellent technical documentation

1. The documentation conforms to legal requirements. It prevents harm to the user or operator, other human beings, to the environment and to equipment.

2. It accurately reflects the technology being described or to be used.

3. The documentation is right for the target group. The style and choice of words are appropriate for the target group.

4. The writing style is clear.

5. Everything you want to say is written out explicitly. Your readers are not kept guessing.

6. Things have exactly one name. Only that name is used.

7. The passive voice is rarely used.

8. Each sentence communicates only one thought.

9. There are no amputated sentences.

10. The conceptual subject of each sentence is placed at the beginning of the sentence.

11. The text is not overwritten.

12. Typographical shortcuts are not used.

13. Examples are real, typical examples.

14. Layout elements are used to structure the texts and to emphasize important items.

15. Layout elements are not overused.

16. The readers can easily find the information they need.

17. The introduction complies with generally accepted guidelines.

18. The description tells the reader everything he or she needs to know.

19. Concrete things are given a concrete name.

Table of contents

1   Develop a clear writing style

Let us begin by taking a look at technical German — the way it often is, with all of its abstractness and awkwardness.

This chapter illustrates a few basic techniques for expressing complex German thoughts in simple, but adequate English. My main recommendation is this: Do not attempt to **directly** formulate complicated German sentences in English.

The experiment would probably fail, and might wind up in a book of amusing mistranslations.

Instead, first rewrite the original text in simple German that is free of jargon. The result is then easy to translate.

Technical documentation must be written in language which is clear, straightforward, to the point, accurate, and brief but adequate.

User documentation is a tool which should enable people to do their job. It must therefore be easy to understand and apply.

Technical English uses language which is **simple**, **direct**, and **easy to understand**.

Good examples

- File not found
- NO STEP
- Bad data

This is not poor style. Quite the opposite, it is appropriate for the purpose and thus perfectly acceptable.

Use simple grammatical structures.
Avoid subordinate clauses (Nebensätze)

Example

Write like this:

Loading a cassette module:
- *Place a new cassette in the cassette module, and lock it into position.*
- *Press the Pump key on the operating panel of the cassette module.*

The cassette module closes automatically and is pumped down.

Keep your sentences short and simple

Example

The following is too long:

Over the last several decades, increasingly exacting demands have been placed on the quality and functionality of electronic components in motor vehicles, and this trend is set to continue.

Divide this into two sentences:

Over the last several decades, increasingly exacting demands have been placed on the quality and functionality of electronic components in motor vehicles. This trend is set to continue.

Avoid substantival expressions

Example

Do not write like this:

The two workers accomplished the division of the material into two piles.
(P&R, p. 79[1])

Rewrite this as follows:

The two workers divided the material into two piles.

The following sentences must be rewritten before they can be translated.

Example

Das Ablösen des Etikettes vom Übergabestempel erfolgt druckluft-unterstützt.

We first rewrite this into simpler German. Imagine explaining the above thought to your young child. What would you say?

Possibly something like this:

Mit Druckluft wird das Etikett vom Übergabestempel abgelöst.

This is easy to translate:

The label is removed from the transfer stamp, by means of compressed air.

---

1   Pauley / Riordan (1993)

Example

Die Zugriffsberechtigungen und die Zuordnung eines Nutzers zu einer dieser Gruppen dürfen auch durch die Systemadministratoren nicht veränderbar sein.

We simplify the text as follows:

Die Systemadministratoren dürfen die Zugriffsberechtigungen und die Zuordnung eines Nutzers zu einer dieser Gruppen nicht verändern können.

This is easy to translate:

The system administrators must not be able to change the access privileges and the assignment of a user to one of these groups.

Exercises

Rewrite and translate the sentences below:

1. *Um ein Verstopfen des Systems zu vermeiden, muss in regelmäßigen Intervallen ein Reinigungvorgang erfolgen.*

2. *Der Reinigungsprozess erfolgt durch das Drehen der Maschine im Servicebetrieb.*

3. *[...] Diese Teile sind im Wesentlichen zusammengefasst im Elektronikschrank.*

4. *Data Warehousing ist hierzulande erst von sehr wenigen Anwendererfahrungen geprägt.*

5. *Neben den eigentlichen Parametern enthalten diese Dateien auch Kommentare, mit denen die Wirkungsweise der einzelnen Werte dargestellt bzw. die für den einzelnen Parameter möglichen Werte angegeben werden.*

6. *Der Menüpunkt Fläche zeigt die Gesamtfläche des aktuellen Raumes, ohne Abzug von Säulenflächen an. Im Textausdruck findet eine Differenzierung statt.*

2   Avoid substantival expressions

In German – especially technical German – nouns are important. This results in text which is very compact. Native speakers of English, in contrast, express themselves in fully written-out sentences, often with verbal phrases. That is, the expressive power of well-written English comes from using **verbs** – not nouns.

Hence, the key to writing excellent technical English is to express the author's intention with as few nouns as possible. Techniques and examples are provided below.

It is tempting to translate substantival German sentences into substantival English ones. However, the result is difficult to read, difficult to understand, and sounds somehow "wrong".

Example

Die Breite des Tisches beträgt 3 Meter.

Problem:

English does not typically use substantival structures like this.

Recommendation:

Do not attempt to translate substantival German texts. First, rewrite the German sentence without the substantivation. Then translate that.

Applying the recommendation:

Der Tisch ist 3 Meter breit.

Good translation:

The table is 3 meters wide.

This is how native speakers of English would express themselves.

Example

Die Anzahl der Teilnehmer ist auf 25 Personen begrenzt.

Recommendation:
Rewrite the German, eliminating the substantivation.

Applying the recommendation:
Nur 25 Personen können/dürfen teilnehmen.

Good translation:
Only 25 Persons can/may participate.

Which helping verb is correct: *can* or *may*? Ask the author to clarify the issue.

Example

Preparation for connecting motor size 63

Recommendation:
Express the noun "preparation" some other way.

Applying the recommendation:
* *Before connecting motor size 63*
* *Before you connect motor size 63*

Example

Grease the pipes prior to reassembly

Recommendation:
Express the noun "reassembly" with a verbal phrase.

Applying the recommendation:
* *Grease the pipes before you reassemble them.*
* *Grease the pipes before reassembling them.*

Note that headings, subheadings and chapter titles are always expressed using the following verbal pattern:

Good example

Aligning the cams

Stylistic trap:
- *Cam alignment*
- *Alignment of the cams*
- *Aligning of the cams*

Good example

Inspecting the machine

Stylistic trap:
- *Machine inspection*
- *Inspection of the machine*
- *Inspecting of the machine*

With headings, subheadings and chapter titles, the stylistic trap is to use a substantival pattern. A native speaker would express these items with a verbal pattern, and would consider a substantival phrase to be too complicated.

Poor example of a heading

Installation of the drive shaft

Recommendation:
Express the noun "installation" as a verb with the "ing" form.

Applying the recommendation:
Installing the drive shaft

Example

Heading in German:
3.2 Kabelüberprüfung

Good example:
3.2 Checking the cable(s)

Exercises

1. *Die Qualität eines optischen Systems wird auch **durch dessen Symmetriezustand** bestimmt.*

2. *Do not route brake cables alongside power cables, since otherwise there is a risk of disrupting brake controllers.*

3. *Research showed the division of waste products into biodegradable and nonbiodegradable substances.* (P&R, p. 77)

4. *The two workers accomplished the division of the material into two piles.* (P&R, p. 79)

5. *Any nonconformance in a safety application which might, for example, cause an airbag to malfunction can have life-threatening consequences for car passengers.*

6. *For a successful business, the satisfaction of the customer's needs at a profit must be done by the company.* (P&R, p. 79)

7. *Speedboat Excellence embodies a comprehensive appreciation of quality relating to products and services, but also to management performance and the quality of the organization as a whole in all areas, with the aim of achieving sustained results and long-term success.*

8. *The capacity for an operator, in one day, for reconditioning plugs, is about 400.* (P&R, p. 79)

9. *To achieve an average failure rate of 500 ppm, corresponding to a 0.05 percent defect probability − i.e. five failures in one million manufactured vehicles − car manufacturers require a defect probability of less than 10 ppm from the system suppliers.*

10. *The program operates at all levels of the organizational structure: on the one hand through the strong commitment and example of management, on the other through continuous implementation and optimization in teams and the contribution of each individual employee.*

11. *The process we use to accomplish these objectives is through the concise description of limitations, the investigation of alternatives, and the establishment of communication channels.* (P&R, p. 79)

3   Use "…-ing" for complex thoughts

The English language has a grammatical device, the gerund, which allows us to express complex ideas very simply.

Examples

- More and more electronic circuits are being built into vehicles, and the demands made of testers are increasing.
- More and more electronic circuits are being built into vehicles. The demands made of testers are increasing.

Problem:

This is choppy and difficult to read.

Recommendation:

Use the pattern … -*ing* for complex thoughts.

Applying the recommendation:

More and more electronic circuits are being built into vehicles, increasing the demands made of testers.

This is easy to read, easy to understand, and allows the sentence to flow.

Example

Der äußerst robuste und schwere Verladekopf drückt die speziell entwickelte Kunststoffdichtung optimal in die Tanköffnung und sorgt somit für eine staubfreie Verladung.

The following translation reads well:

The extremely robust and heavy loading nozzle presses the specially developed plastic seal optimally into the tank opening, ensuring dust-free loading.

Do not write:

The extremely robust and heavy loading nozzle presses the specially developed plastic seal optimally into the tank opening and ensures dust-free loading.

Example

*Benutzt man statt Gleichstrom Wechselstrom, so bezeichnet man den im Wechselstromkreis gegebenen Widerstand mit Z **und** erhält für die obige Grundformel ...*

The following translation reads well:

If AC current is used instead of DC, then the resistance in the AC circuit is designated as Z, resulting *in the following for the above basic equation ...*

Do not write:

If AC current is used instead of DC, then the resistance in the AC circuit is designated as Z, and results in the following for the above basic equation ...

Exercises

1. *Yachting Excellence is revolutionizing the boating industry and opens up new worlds of experience to spoiled yacht lovers.*

2. *Check the cable before you check the electrodes.*

3. *The light sensors are in the shadows, that makes measurement easier.*

4. *Die Umstellung der Bordspannung auf 24 V verursacht weitere Probleme.*

4   Avoid the passive voice

Native speakers of English would not hesitate to tell someone exactly what to do. This is not considered to be impolite, and it adds clarity to technical writing. Many German sentences using the passive voice should be expressed in English as a command.

On the other hand, I wish to emphasize that the passive voice has its place; it should not be rejected categorically. In particular, it is entirely appropriate in system descriptions. Such manuals and texts explain how something works, they do not tell an operator how to do his or her work.

Recommendation

Use passive only:
* if the agent is totally unimportant, e.g.:
  Robots are used for repetitive activities.
* to emphasize the important thing, e.g.:
  Ink droplets *are ejected from the nozzle at high speed.*

In users' manuals, there is always an agent for every activity. Name it explicitly. Do not keep the reader guessing who is to do the activity.

Following this rule often makes translating easier. German texts frequently use the passive voice, even when instructing the reader how to do something. Our translation is very readable if we translate the instruction using the imperative form rather than the passive voice.

Example

Durch Eingabe eines zweistelligen Parameters wird die Zeit vorgewählt.

Good translation:

Select a time by entering a two-digit parameter.

Exercises

Rewrite the sentences below, which are part of users' manuals. For these exercises, simply "invent" any missing details which you might need to make fully useful statements:

1. *Ensure that sufficient storage space is allocated.*

2. *Program execution must be halted if measurement errors are discovered.*

3. *Keeping a desired overpressure is accomplished by using a pressure-drop control valve.* (P&R, p. 78)

4. *When the display has been noted and is no longer needed, press the R/S button to proceed with the program.* (P&R, p. 78)

5. *Ist der Filz verschmutzt, wird er abgezogen und durch einen neuen ersetzt.*

5   Each sentence should communicate only one thought

The German language has grammatical structures which allow readers to understand long sentences; English does not. It is "short of breath", so to speak.

For this reason, a good general rule is to express only one thought in each sentence. The writer's task is two-fold. He or she must recognize sentences which contain more than one thought. An example is *"Die Umstellung der Bordspannung auf 24 V verursacht weitere Probleme"*. This states both that the board voltage was converted to 24 V and that this conversion is causing additional problems.

At the same time, the writer should avoid formulating a series of short, staccato-like sentences. Sometimes, the best solution is to use the gerund (see Chapter 3 Use ... *-ing* for complex thoughts).

Example

Do not attempt to translate the following in a single sentence:

Die einzelnen per Tastendruck abrufbaren Menüs entnehmen Sie bitte folgenden Bildern.

Damit bei Wechsel der Flaschengröße seitens des Abfüllbetriebes der Strahlengang angepasst werden kann, ist eine Justiervorrichtung erforderlich, die den Strahl in der Messbox genau an die zu analysierende Flaschengröße anpasst.

Exercises

1. *Unter dem Menüpunkt Kontrolle in der seitlichen Menüleiste können Sie schon erfasste Wand- und Diagonallängen durch eine Kontrollmessung überprüfen.*

2. *Empfehlenswert ist eine Kontrollmessung dann, wenn Sie unsicher sind ob die Messungen mit dem DATA DITTO ordnungsgemäß ausgeführt worden sind, oder nach Abschluss eines Raumes, um sicher zu sein, dass Sie keine Messfehler gemacht haben.*

3. *Der gemessene Wert wird im Eingabefeld, der vom Programm errechnete Wert darunter angezeigt.*

4. *The increasing amount of in-boat electronics is causing ever greater complexity in terms of the interactions of individual components and is the biggest challenge facing the boat industry's entire value chain.*

5. *The Augsburg is a high-quality press the price is beyond our budget at the present time.*

6. *The TG4 has a stainless steel front this will help in cleaning the oven.*

6   Avoid amputated sentences

Technical texts are often written in a shortened form. Two common forms of amputated sentences are:

- thoughts expressed merely as a noun in parentheses;
- substantival wordings.

Thoughts expressed merely as a noun in parentheses

Example

Mit der Taste FAST kann die TEACH-Geschwindigkeit umgeschaltet werden. (Funktion, wie Manuell-Betrieb.)

Recommendation:
Fully write out the thought in parentheses.

Applying the recommendation:
Mit der Taste FAST kann die TEACH-Geschwindigkeit umgeschaltet werden. Dafür verwendet man die Funktion zur Geschwindigkeitsumschaltung, die auch im Manuell-Betrieb zur Verfügung steht.

Translation:
The button FAST can be used to switch the TEACH speed. For this, use the function for changing the speed which is available in manual mode.

Substantival wordings

How do you translate sentences such as the following?

* *Durch Drücken der Reset-Taste ...*
* *Nach Erreichen der Obergrenze ...*
* *Programmabbruch mit der Abort-Taste*

Example

Programmabbruch mit der Abort-Taste

Suggestion:

1. Write a fully written-out German sentence:

Wenn Sie die Ausführung des Programms abbrechen möchten, dann drücken Sie die Abort-Taste.

2. Translate that into English:

If you want to abort program execution, then press the Abort key.

This is even worse if the sentence uses the passive voice, or is substantival:

* *Durch Drücken der Reset-Taste wird zum Hauptmenü zurückgekehrt.*
* *Durch Drücken der Reset-Taste Rückkehr zum Hauptmenü.*

If it is clear that the user is to do something, then write the sentence as a command:

Drücken Sie die Reset-Taste, um zum Hauptmenü zu gelangen.

Press the Reset key to return to the main menu.

Exercises

Try to translate the following sentences into English. What will you have to do?

1. *Bei Verwendung der Schrittgröße 4 sollte immer dann in das special-Menü zurückgekehrt werden, wenn mit Sicherheit davon auszugehen ist, dass das Ölfilter verschmutzt oder beschädigt ist. Ansonsten Verletzungsgefahr!*

2. *Auswahl der Leerfahrfunktion generell nur bei vorheriger Entfernung aller Flaschen vom Förderband möglich! Sonst Flaschenstau!*

3. *Die Voraussetzung für die Benutzung der Maus ist jedoch die Auswahl des Treibers L1 durch den autorisierten Benutzer (Punkt Maustreiber im Menü Systemeinstellungen). Bei Verwendung des falschen Treibers bzw. Nichtauswahl eines Treibers erfolgt Fehlfunktion der Maus. Nach Auswahl des Treibers Warmstart des Rechners erforderlich (Reset).*

4. *Rückspulen des Bandes durch gleichzeitiges Drücken der Tasten Back und Tape. Hörbares Bandendegeräusch nach Erreichen des Bandendes dann Stop drücken.*

5. *Verlassen dieses Eingabefensters nur nach Anwahl der einzelnen Optionen möglich (oder Cancel drücken).*

6. *Der Filename wird nach Drücken von Return in der Titelleiste bestätigt.*

7. *Es wird nur jeder zweite Anschluss aktiviert (trotz Unterschreitens der Höchstteilnehmerzahl).*

8. *Im Eingabefenster wird das Passwort generell zweimal eingegeben.*

9. *Bestätigen der Eingabe mit Return.*

10. *Nach Erreichen des Sollwertes wird die Anlage abgeschaltet.*

7 Decompress compact wordings

In Munich, instructions on how to react to emergencies are posted in the subway cars. These instructions include the following warning:

Example

Schwellenhöhe beachten!

Poor translation:
Heed threshold height!

The problem:
The German sentence is an overly compact way of warning people to not underestimate the distance to the ground. The poor translation, *"Heed threshold height!"*, does not tell people what they are supposed to do.

Recommendation:
Determine what the author means. Then write out what he or she means, in full detail. **Tell people exactly what to do!**

Applying the recommendation:
The ground might be very far down. So be very careful when you leave the subway and step down to the ground. Do not fall and break your legs!

(Of course, space for this message might be limited.)

Example

Please take note of the reduced grease utilization period of the ball bearings after storage periods exceeding one year.

Recommendation:
Tell people exactly what to do!

Example

Comply with the wiring instructions issued by the manufacturer when motors are po-wered by inverters.

Recommendation:

"When motors are powered by inverters" is the primary consideration here. If the motors are not powered by inverters, **the reader can ignore the entire sentence**. So give him or her the decision structure **first**.

Try to imagine how Walt Disney would present this information in one of his parks. Walt was a genius at clarity. He would probably shout: *Are the motors powered by inverters? Yes? Then comply with the manufacturer's wiring instructions!*

Applying the recommendation:

If the motors are powered by inverters, comply with the manufacturer's wiring instructions.

Note:

The statement is incomplete. Which manufacturer does the author mean? The manufacturer of the motors, or of the inverters?

Exercises

1. *Please take note of the reduced grease utilization period of the ball bearings after storage periods exceeding one year.*

2. *Die Transistoren T14 und T9 sehen ähnlich aus, Vertauschungsgefahr!*

3. *Save the data if necessary.*

4. *Wasserstand kontrollieren, evtl. nachfüllen.*

5. *The motor must be dried if the insulation resistance is not adequate.*

8   First word = conceptual subject

The following discussion of word order relates only to **technical** English. In everyday English, word order can be varied in more ways than I discuss below. This chapter suggests a subset of options for word order in technical writing.

In German, word order is used flexibly as a mechanism for emphasizing whatever is important. In technical English, we can add considerable clarity to our writing by adhering to **standard word order**:

Subject – verb – object

I wish to stress the advantages of standard word order, especially since German is so different. Germans who write in English or translate into English might not be quite aware of how important this issue is.

Let us begin by considering the following sentence:

Example

Das Herzstück des Systems ist der Hebearm.

Poor English:
The heart of the system is the lifting arm.

When you begin a sentence with: "The heart ...", a native speaker of the language will expect you to talk about some biological heart. When he or she discovers the sentence is actually about a lifting arm, then the person will be confused.

Recommendation:
1.   Identify who or what is doing something in each sentence. That is the **conceptual subject** of the sentence.
2.   Make sure this conceptual subject is the grammatical subject of the sentence. Rewrite the text if it is not.
3.   Place this grammatical subject at the very beginning of the sentence.

Applying the recommendation:
The lifting arm is the heart of the system.

This is easy to understand.

Word order is actually much more complicated. The fundamental rule is:

Always keep the main message together. Never provide details within the main message

Example

A series resonant circuit shunts as described above exactly one frequency to ground.

Where do we put details?

We place details either **before** or **after** the main message, like this:

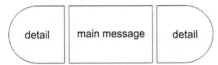

When do details go before the main message, when afterwards?

If a detail is important, then it goes first; for example:

As described above, a series resonant circuit shunts exactly one frequency to ground.

If the detail is unimportant, then it goes last; for example:

A series resonant circuit shunts exactly one frequency to ground, as described above.

Word order also depends on what part of the sentence is shorter, the main message or details. Put the shorter part **first**. For example, consider the following statement:

Example

*I enjoyed a long, pleasant meal and then met my wife for a movie at our local cinema **despite the thunderstorm**.*

Native speakers of English would not use such word order. Here, the detail is much shorter than the main message, and we would put that first:

***Despite the thunderstorm**, I enjoyed a long, pleasant meal and then met my wife for a movie at our local cinema.*

Do not put the shorter part at the end of a sentence, as in:

*Although our neighbors had a party in the garden that lasted well into the night and played music all night that I cannot stand, **I slept well**.*

Rewrite this as follows:

***I slept well**, although our neighbors had a party in the garden that lasted well into the night and played music all night that I cannot stand.*

Exercises

1. *The responsibility for overriding blood pressure monitoring lies with the physician.*
2. *Die Befehle werden jeden Samstag ausgeführt.*
3. *Die Namen der Maschinen werden jetzt im Eingabefenster eingegeben.*
4. *Click in the main window on the Align tab.*
5. *Data between two computers is transmitted by modems.* (P&R, p. 74)
6. *In service mode, the status of the inlets and outlets can be checked.*
7. *After the fault is eliminated, a reference run must be made.*
8. *Vor Eingabe der benötigten Zahlen liest der Benutzer die Anweisung durch.*

9 Do not overwrite

The readers of technical texts are paid to do a demanding job, such as operating complex machinery.We can make their work easier for them by being **direct** and **brief**.

Example

Install the parts as demonstrated by the following illustration.

Recommendation:
Reduce this sentence to the bare essentials.

Suggestion:
Install the parts as shown:

Identify words that are not saying anything, such as:

* ... die **jeweils** aktuelle Maske
* ... die **einzelnen** Drähte
* ... in terms of the interactions of **individual** components

Do not translate them.

Exercises

1. *In dem Feld Dateinamen wird der programmintern angelegte Dateiname für den jeweiligen Gebäudeabschnitt zur Information angezeigt.*
2. *In caring for your blender, you should remember to care for it like you would any other electrical appliance.* (P&R, p. 82)
3. *The plate is supported again by a thick wire that extends down into a connecting pin in the base, and the exact position of the pin is the pin next to the notch in the base.* (P&R, p. 82)

10 Resist the temptation to use typographical shortcuts

Developers have a habit of using shortcuts. Chapter 6 Avoid amputated sentences dealt with some of these time-saving devices.

Authors sometimes use typographical shortcuts, in order to accelerate the writing process. In the interest of clear communication, it is better to write out full sentences.

Examples

- *The original/copy can now be loaded.*
- *Use this application to store/back up the files.*

Recommendation:

Write out exactly what you mean.

Applying the recommendation:

- *You can now load the original or copy.*
- *Use this application to store or back up the files.*

11 Address your reader directly

German authors often prefer to state commands indirectly. In English, we would never do this. Native speakers of English do not hesitate to directly tell people what to do.

General statement instead of a command

Example

It is essential to comply with the safety notes in Section 2 during installation!

The reader is supposed to do something; so write this thought as a command.

Suggestion:
- *Comply with the safety notes in Section 2 during installation.*
- *During installation, you absolutely must comply with the safety notes in Section 2.*

"Sollen" instead of a command

Example

*Der Cursor **soll** jetzt links von dem Eingabefenster stehen.*

The author is probably trying to tell the reader what to do.

In English, we would express this simply as a command:
- *Place the cursor to the left of the input window.*
- *Make sure the cursor is to the left of the input window.*

The passive voice instead of a command

Example

Der Dichtring wird gereinigt und mit wenig Dichtungsfett eingefettet.

In English, we would say something like this:
Clean the sealing ring and lubricate it with just a little sealing grease.

Make it very clear who is to do something:
If the agent is unimportant, use the passive voice.

If the reader is supposed to do something, express the thought as a command.

Example

Anmerkung: Ein Vertauschen der Farbanschlüsse der Krokodilklemmen - schwarz auf rot oder umgekehrt - sollte vermieden werden.

Recommendation:
Tell the reader (the user of a device) exactly what to do.

Applying the recommendation:
Comment: Do not swap the alligator clips. Do not connect the black one where the red one goes, or vice versa.

Example

Eine Elektrodenüberprüfung ist erst nach einer Kabelüberprüfung sinnvoll.

Recommendation:
Tell the reader exactly what to do.

Applying the recommendation:
- *Check the cable before checking the electrodes.*
- *Check the cable. Then check the electrodes.*
- *1. Check the cable.*
  2. Check the electrodes.

Example

Check whether the motor has absorbed moisture as a result of being stored for a long period. To do this, measure insulation resistance (measuring voltage 500 V).

Recommendation:

Simplify this as radically as possible:

- Imagine you are standing next to the technician; tell him exactly what to do in simple words.
- Eliminate the parentheses.

Applying the recommendation:

Has the motor been stored for a long time and become moist? Find out, by measuring the insulation resistance. Use a measuring voltage of 500 V.

Exercises

Translate the following sentences:

1. *Nun wird der Lautsprecher montiert, dazu soll als erstes die Anschluss-litzen 48 und 49 auf die richtige Länge von jeweils 60 mm gebracht werden.*

2. *Jetzt wird die andere Schutzfolie abgezogen und nun kann der Laut-sprecher auf die Leiterplatte geklebt werden.*

3. *Compliance with the safety precautions of Chapter 2 is necessary.*

4. *Seals must be glued in on one side.*

Rewrite the following **in German**, telling people exactly what to do when. Be specific, not vague. For example, what does "bei unmmittelbarer Gefahr" really mean? Then translate this version into English. You will probably notice how easy that is now.[2]

Verhalten bei Betriebsstörungen

1. *Bei allen außergewöhnlichen Vorkommnissen bitte* **Ruhe bewahren** *und die Anweisungen des Personals abwarten.*

2. *Das Erlöschen der Beleuchtung in den Wagen bedeutet keine Gefahr.*

3. *Bei Rauchentwicklung oder Brand außerhalb von Haltestellen Notbremse erst nach Einfahrt in die nächste Haltestelle betätigen.* **Bei unmittelbarer Gefahr** *Feuer bekämpfen;* **Feuerlöscher** *befindet sich unter dem gekennzeichneten Sitz.*

4. *Bei Halt außerhalb von Haltestellen* **nicht ohne Aufforderung durch das Personal aussteigen;** *eigenmächtiges Aussteigen ist* **lebensgefährlich.**

5. *Fordert das Personal zum Aussteigen außerhalb von Haltestellen auf, so ist es zweckmäßig, sich von der Türschwelle sitzend herabzulassen.* **Nicht auf die Stromabnehmer treten.** *Das Personal übernimmt die Führung zur nächsten Haltestelle.*

---

2   The text is taken from the safety precautions posted in subway cars in Munich.

12 Be careful with noun-verb combinations

Written German often uses combinations of nouns and verbs. When Germans write in English, a common problem is that **the writer selects the wrong verb**. The result is difficult to understand – and embarrassing for the author.

My experience is that even Germans with an excellent command of the English language often have this problem.

Example

Recommendation:
Use a verb, rather than a noun–verb combination:

… in Abzug zu bringen.

= to place into deduction? to put into deduction? to bring into deduction?

Applying the recommendation:
to deduct

Example

Die Betonung auf xyz legen.

= to lay emphasis on? To put emphasis on? To place emphasis on?

Applying the recommendation:
to emphasize

Exercise

Express the following in English:

Vor der jeweiligen Geräte-Gleichstrom-Speisungseinheit findet eine Wandlung vom zugeführten Versorgungsnetz mit Wechselspannung (110 V/60 Hz oder 230 V/50 Hz) statt.

13   Unfold your sentences

German writers often place a great deal of information before the noun. This is totally foreign to English.

Good example

He was the man who gave me the advice that saved my life.

Avoid the temptation to create a compact structure, such as:
The life-saving man ...

In English, that sounds very strange.

In many cases, the best advice is to write **several** English sentences for one German sentence. **Use plenty of words,** to express exactly what the author wants to say **in simple language**. Do not use compact wordings.

Exercises

Express the following in English:

1. *Die in einer Reihe von internationalen Studien vielfach belegte Wirksamkeit des Mittels ist durch die Untersuchungen von Prof. Schneider – noch einmal – zweifelsfrei bewiesen worden.*

2. *Dabei war nicht vorgegeben, jedoch erwünscht, mit einer relativ großen Versuchspersonenanzahl Aussagen in Richtung möglichst "hoher, statistischer Signifikanz" zu treffen.*

14   Use simple verbs

In a study of technical texts written in English, I discovered that overly complicated verbs are often used. This tends to complicate the communication process. The problem is even worse when the readers are not native speakers of English.

An additional difficulty is that mastery of technical English is required to select the **proper** complicated verb. German writers should therefore use the simplest verb that explains the situation correctly. Some technical matters can be expressed with "to have" or "to be"; try them before you make your writing complicated.

Example
Beim Transport stellt das Gewicht des Förderarms das größte Problem dar.

Poor translation:
During transportation, the weight of the lifting arm depicts the major problem.

"To depict" is wrong in the given technical context. It is misleading and much too complicated.

Recommendation:
Use the simplest verb that accurately expresses the author's intention. For the above sentence, translate *darstellen* simply as *is*.

Applying the recommendation:
During transportation, the weight of the lifting arm is the major problem.

This sentence is easy to understand.

Example
A transformer may be present in the VS system.

Recommendation:
Simplify *"be present"*.

Applying the recommendation:
Your VS system might have a transformer.

Example

Comply with the wiring instructions issued by the manufacturer.

Recommendation:
Sometimes, the verb can be eliminated completely.

Applying the recommendation:
Comply with the manufacturer's wiring instructions.

Exercises

1. *Based on the Total Quality Management system, Speedboat Excellence constitutes an integrated approach for efficiently ensuring the quality of products and services with a zero-defect objective consonant with customer requirements in the speedboat industry.*

2. *The sensors are located in the tank.*

3. *Erst nach Vorliegen eines ausreichenden Behälter-Füllstandes kann mit der Flaschenreinigung begonnen werden.*

15 Since X, Y ...

Technical translators and writers almost always write about complex technical matters. Many times, one thing is the cause of something else; and the cause–effect relationship may be essential to understanding the situation. The writing can be impossible to understand if **cause** and **effect** are not kept apart. In such situations, the secret is to clearly identify and differentiate cause and effect.

Example

Consider the following:

Since the transistor polarity is vitally important, especially for the types 2N2222, 2N4381, 2N5509 and others, the patterns on the component side must be checked ...

This is difficult to understand, for two reasons:

1. In English, a structure such as *"Since X, Y"* is **inherently confusing**. English is "short of breath", so to speak. Native speakers expect authors to structure their writing in a clear, logical manner. In the above example, we must remember *"Since the transistor polarity ..."*, while reading *"the patterns on the component side..."*.

2. The above sentence is based on the pattern *"Since X, Y"*. The reader needs the comma, in order to clearly separate X from Y. However, the author lists transistor types, which are also separated by commas. So it is difficult to find the comma which separates X from Y.

Recommendation:

Rewrite such thoughts as two sentences. Remove *"since"* from the first sentence. Start the second sentence with *"Thus"*, or *"Hence"*, or "For this reason".

Applying the recommendation:

The transistor polarity is vitally important, especially for the types 2N2222, 2N4381, 2N5509 and others. Thus, the patterns on the component side must be checked ...

By the way, this can be made easier to read by adding parentheses:

The transistor polarity is vitally important (especially for the types 2N2222, 2N4381, 2N5509 and others). Thus, the patterns on the component side must be checked ...

16 Express concrete ideas in a concrete way, especially if people are involved

English is a **specific** language. Thoughts about people should be expressed in the form:

Who is doing what?

Example

Es findet ein Umdenken statt.

Poor translation:
A rethinking takes place.

Problem:
Native speakers of English will not understand this.

Recommendation:
Express this as a **practical thought**, about people and their attitudes.

Applying the recommendation:
• *People's attitudes about [retirement …] are changing.*
• Or even: *People are changing their attitudes about [retirement …].*

This is easy to understand.

When we rewrite the sentence clearly, we notice that **information is missing** (attitudes about what?).

I experience frequently that missing information must be added when thoughts are formulated clearly. The result is an expression which communicates the author's full intention.

Remember that English is a specific language. This is especially true with regard to technical English. Tell your reader exactly **what to do**. Communicate the author's full intention.

Exercises

1. *Der Vorschlag ist gekommen ...*

2. *Dies ist – vermutlich! – eine Aufforderung zum Handeln.*

3. *"'Es gibt keine grundlegende Abkehr von diesem Kurs', erklärten ihre Sprecher Andrea Nahles und Michael Müller in Berlin"* (Süddeutsche Zeitung for May 26, 2005)

17   Your sentences should flow

Technical writing does not need to be aesthetically pleasing. However, the communication process can be facilitated by writing sentences which are easy to read, rather than choppy and bloated.

In many cases, overloaded German sentences should be expressed as several sentences in English. Short, choppy sentences can often be joined together.

Exercises

1. *Sie können die Ausmaße von Türen ändern (Breite ändern, Höhe ändern) oder die Lage in einer Wand neu bestimmen (horizontal bzw. vertikal verschieben).*

2. *Bei Anwendung eines 5-Ω drahtgewickelten (Präzisions-) bzw. eines 75-Ω NTC-Widerstands (Baureihe RW 450 bzw. 324) bzw. bei Einsatz in rauer Umgebung ...*

3. *The computer is a Model 1. It is 7 years old. It does not have sufficient RAM. No new programs will run on it.*

4. *The taste test is important in food development. The test is run by lab technicians. The technicians are supervised by a sensory evaluator. (P&R, p. 82)*

18   Use commas properly

Commas are used to help the reader understand the author's intentions. In English writing, commas are placed according to rules completely unlike those which apply in German.

The fundamental principle is to add a comma whenever a competent speaker would instinctively pause when saying a given sentence aloud.

Never use commas as you would in German

Examples

Never write:
- *She said, the motorcycle was too expensive.*
- *He claimed, the participants arrived late.*

The correct punctuation is as follows:
- *She said the motorcycle was too expensive.*
- *He claimed the participants arrived late.*

Separate subordinate clauses with commas

Examples
- *When biased properly, the transistor works like a switch.*
- *Everyone looked forward to the party, although the planning had been chaotic.*

The commas make these sentences easier to read and understand. Consider the example, "When biased properly, the transistor works like a switch". Without the comma – "When biased properly the transistor works like a switch" – the clear structure is lost, forcing the reader to work too hard.

Subordinate clauses in the middle of a sentence must be surrounded by commas

Examples

- Mr. Jones, everybody's favorite teacher, was unable to attend the assembly.
- The price of gasoline, experts agree, will increase steadily in future years.
- The New York Times, the most respected newspaper in the United States, will be increasing its subscription rates as of January 1, 2006.

Insert commas after "hence", "thus", or "therefore" whenever a sentence begins with one of these words

Examples

- Hence, the printer failed to work properly.
- Thus, the diameter is directly related to the circumference.
- Therefore, the asylum-seeker will be deported.

Separate a series of adjectives with commas

Examples

- *Everyone admired her beautiful, sleek, fascinating car.*
- *They liked the fast, powerful, expensive boat.*

**If you write "and" at the end of a series of adjectives,
do not insert a comma before the word "and":**
Do you remember the hazy, lazy, crazy and humid days of summer?

Do not write:
Do you remember the hazy, lazy, crazy, and humid days of summer?

If possible, insert only one comma
per sentence

Examples

Typical problem cases:
- *Thus, the diameter is directly related to the circumference, although the exact relationship is unknown.*
- *If possible, examine the consumption of flour in Third-World countries, but it might be difficult to find relevant data.*

**Often, the solution is to divide the statement into two sentences.
Here are examples, using the above sentences:**
- *Thus, the diameter is directly related to the circumference. However, the exact relationship is unknown.*
- *If possible, examine the consumption of flour in Third-World Countries. However, it might be difficult to find relevant data.*

Ignore this rule if it makes the sentence difficult to understand

Exercises

Add or delete commas, as required. Also add any other punctuation marks which you feel might be appropriate.

1. *This section shows a template to store a routing tree to the ABC database by using the XYZ batch interface.*

2. *The thresholds must be combined making sure that only one threshold can be reached at a certain time.*

3. *He claimed, the best essay was submitted by your sister.*

4. *For a description of the monitor settings see section 5.8.7 "Rate Plan for the Discount feature".*

5. *Three accumulators count the administrator's CPU usage as follows.*

6. *In my opinion the publishing date should be moved up but I realize this may cause hardship for some people.*

7. *She said, the work must be done whether you like it or not.*

8. *Paul Jones the owner of a large luxurious sophisticated yacht a classic Fedship from the Netherlands arrived at the port on time.*

9. *This section provides a functional description of the Discount feature and shows the corresponding service data.*

10. *For the SuperMFJ feature the same conditions apply as for the ARkE feature (see above).*

19   Use hyphens properly

Hyphens **are** used in English writing. However, the rules which apply are totally different than the German rules.

Never use hyphens as you would in German

Example

Never write:
- *Enter your name in the name-field.*
- *We all attended the Christmas-party.*
- *The PC-printer is not working correctly.*

The correct punctuation is as follows:
- *Enter your name in the name field* (or *Name field*).
- *We all attended the Christmas party.*
- *The PC printer is not working correctly.*

Place a hyphen between an amount and the unit

Example

She purchased a 9-volt battery.
(NOT: *9-volt-battery* or *9 volt battery*!)

We were amazed by the 400-pound elephant.
(NOT: *400-pound-elephant*!)

Use hyphens to clarify what an adjective is modifying

Without the proper punctuation, a reader might not know what an adjective is modifying: the word which follows immediately after it or the subject of the sentence.

Example

Consider the following:

The hot water faucet is broken.

This is confusing. What is hot, the water or the faucet? There are two possibilities:

- The water is hot; i.e.:
  The hot-water faucet is broken.
- The faucet is hot; i.e.:
  The hot water faucet is broken.

Note that in accordance with the first rule we cannot write:

The hot water-faucet is broken.

Example

Don't touch the red hot anvil.

This is confusing. Does the author mean:

Don't touch the red, hot anvil.

Of course not. Thus, a hyphen is required:

Don't touch the red-hot anvil.

Further examples

- *The men repaired the cold water pipe.*
- *People should invest money in private old age insurance.*

**Do you notice the confusion in these sentences? Is the pipe cold?
Is the insur-ance old? These sentences must be corrected as follows:**

- *The men repaired the cold-water pipe.*
- *People should invest money in private old-age insurance.*

**Note: The second rule is actually an application of the third one.
Consider the following, with the wrong punctuation:**

She purchased a 9 volt battery.

**If we read this very quickly, we might think the author was being
sloppy and meant nine batteries. Also, unless we know that
9 modifies volt, we might wonder what a "volt battery" is.
Again, with improper punctuation:**

We were amazed by the 400 pound elephant.

Does the author somehow mean 400 elephants? And what is a "pound elephant"?

Exercises

Correct anything that might be wrong.

1. *The problem, however, cannot be solved as described in the e-mail-
   message.*
2. *The user's name must be entered in the Name-Field.*
3. *In my opinion the printing-date should be pushed back. However this
   could cause hardship for some people.*
4. *Depending on the noise level, the customer must take all required
   steps to protect operating personnel in accordance with noise
   protection regulations and standards.*
5. *The PC-cable is broken.*
6. *The radio needs new 1½ volt batteries, I believe.*
7. *The 4-liter-hat is too big for my head.*
8. *I talk on my handy all the time since I have this flat-rate.*

Wrap-up exercises

The following exercises put it all together. Here, you must decide for yourself which stylistic recommendations are relevant. In section A, make any and all corrections that may be needed.

Improve the following sentences

1. *We must inform each employee that she must fill out a W-4-form. (P&R, p. 83)*
2. *There are five basic requirements that a software must fulfill.*
3. *It is maintained by the user that …*
4. *The user must fill in the required informations in the field Mask-name.*
5. *It is believed that …*
6. *Your complaint has been received by our company, and …*
7. *By entering a two-digit parameter, the time is selected*
8. *After the time "dup2" runs out, the connection to the remote-station is built up.*

Translate the following sentences into English

1. *Nach erfolgter Prüfung seiner Login-Kennung übernimmt der Benutzer Administratoraufgaben.*
2. *Die Überprüfung der in das OMC noch nicht übertragenen Datenbits erfordert einen zweiten Eintrag in das Heimatregister.*
3. *Das bereits vorher eingegebene Beispiel soll in der Datei "Field lengths" abgespeichert werden.*
4. *Der neue Mikroprozessor-Chip ist in 0,25-µm-Technik realisiert.*
5. *Die Schnittstelle ist im vorliegenden Gerät als leistungsfähiges 320-bps-Ausgabeport realisiert.*

6. *Die Rechte eines Administrators erhält der Benutzer erst nach Prüfung seiner Login-Kennung*

7. *"'Es gibt keine grundlegende Abkehr von diesem Kurs', erklärten ihre Sprecher Andrea Nahles und Michael Müller in Berlin".* (Süddeutsche Zeitung for May 26, 2005)

8. *Es findet ein Umdenken statt.*

Suggested solutions for the exercises

Chapter 1: Develop a clear writing style

1. *Um ein Verstopfen des Systems zu vermeiden, muss in regelmäßigen Intervallen ein Reinigungvorgang erfolgen.*

   Is this part of a user manual or of a system description? If the statement is something the user is supposed to do, then it should be written as a direct command:

   To avoid clogging, clean the system regularly.

   If the statement is part of a system description, then write:

   The system must be cleaned regularly, to avoid clogging.

2. *Der Reinigungsprozess erfolgt durch das Drehen der Maschine im Servicebetrieb.*

   If we know that the operator (the reader) is supposed to do this, we can write:

   To clean the machine, rotate it in service mode.

   This statement can be simplified by putting some of the information in a subheading:

   Cleaning the machine
   In service mode, rotate it.

   If the sentence is not something the reader is to do, but rather is part of a system description, then the passive voice is appropriate:

   The machine is cleaned by rotating it in service mode.

3. *[...] Diese Teile sind im Wesentlichen zusammengefasst im Elektronik-Schrank.*

What does "im Wesentlichen" mean? The trap here is to translate the sentence literally:

These parts are essentially summarized in the electronics cabinet.

This is garbage! The correct translation, based on an understanding of what "im Wesentlichen" means:

Most of these parts are located in the electronics cabinet.

4. *Data Warehousing ist hierzulande erst von sehr wenigen Anwendererfahrungen geprägt.*

The only way to express this correctly is to carefully consider what the author is trying to say:

Few Germans are familiar with data warehousing.

5. *Neben den eigentlichen Parametern enthalten diese Dateien auch Kommentare, mit denen die Wirkungsweise der einzelnen Werte dargestellt bzw. die für den einzelnen Parameter möglichen Werte angegeben werden.*

What are "eigentliche Parameter"? This is common jargon in technical German, and it is very important to recognize this. Does the meaning of the sentence change if we leave "eigentlich" out? No! Hence, for the translation simply ignore this word. The same is true for the word "einzeln".

These files specify the parameters, with comments on permissible values and the effects of these values.

Why did I not begin the sentence with "In addition to the parameters, ..."? Because it is about **files**; for clarity, the sentence should begin with "These files ...".

6. *Der Menüpunkt Fläche zeigt die Gesamtfläche des aktuellen Raumes, ohne Abzug von Säulenflächen an. Im Textausdruck findet eine Differenzierung statt.*

   Again, the trap is to translate the German sentence literally:

   The menu item Area displays the total area of the current room, including the area of columns. In the printout, a differentiation takes place.

   You can avoid this trap by asking yourself what "Im Textausdruck findet eine Differenzierung statt" means. For the printout, the areas of the columns are subtracted from the total area. For the translation, say exactly that:

   The menu item Area displays the total area of the current room, including the area of columns. For the printout, the areas of the columns are subtracted from the total area.

Chapter 2: Avoid substantival expressions

1. *Die Qualität eines optischen Systems wird auch durch dessen Symmetriezustand bestimmt.*

   The trap is: How do we express "Symmetriezustand"? "symmetry status"? "symmetry state"? "state of symmetry"? ... The problem is that none of these expressions are common in technical English, so a native speaker would probably be confused by them. The solution is to express "Symmetriezustand" with a phrase:

   The quality of an optical system is partially determined by how symmetrical it is.

   Native speakers of English would express themselves this way.

2. *Die Qualität eines optischen Systems wird auch durch dessen Symmetriezustand bestimmt.*

The trap is: How do we express "Symmetriezustand"? "symmetry status"? "symmetry state"? "state of symmetry"? ... The problem is that none of these expressions are common in technical English, so a native speaker would probably be confused by them. The solution is to express "Symmetriezustand" with a phrase:

The quality of an optical system is partially determined by how symmetrical it is.

Native speakers of English would express themselves this way.

3. *Do not route brake cables alongside power cables, since otherwise there is a risk of disrupting brake controllers.*

The expression "there is a risk of" is too complicated. For one thing, most sentences beginning with "there is/there are" should be rewritten in a simpler, direct way. In addition, the noun "risk" can be eliminated; the result is a clear statement.

Do not route brake cables alongside power cables. Otherwise, the brake controllers could be disrupted.

Note that the first sentence is written in the imperative form. For stylistic consistency, the second sentence should also address the reader directly:

Do not route brake cables alongside power cables. Otherwise, you might disrupt the brake controllers.

4. *Research showed the division of waste products into biodegradable and nonbiodegradable substances.* (P&R, p. 77)

Always eliminate nouns whenever you can. The result is an English sentence that is easy to read and understand. The more nouns you can eliminate, the better. Here, "the division" obviously should be removed:

Research showed that waste products can be divided into biodegradable and nonbiodegradable substances.

5. *The two workers accomplished the division of the material into two piles.*

   Again, simplify by eliminating a noun:
   The two workers divided the material into two piles.

   If the workers' **ability** is important:
   The two workers were able to divide the material into two piles.

6. *Any nonconformance in a safety application which might, for example, cause an airbag to malfunction can have life-threatening consequences for car passengers.*

   What are "life-threatening consequences"? Clearly, here we are talking about dying. An unpleasant subject, so it is tempting to use a fancy expression. Here is my suggestion:
   If a car's safety feature were to malfunction, causing e.g. an airbag to fail, the passengers might die.

   Technical English should always be as specific as possible. What happens when an airbag fails? It does not inflate; we could say that:
   If a car's safety feature were to malfunction, causing e.g. an airbag to not inflate, then the passengers might die.

7. *For a successful business, the satisfaction of the customer's needs at a profit must be done by the company.* (P&R, p. 79)

   Think about the author's intention; then eliminate nouns and simplify verbs:
   Successful businesses satisfy the customer's needs while making a profit.

8. *Speedboat Excellence embodies a comprehensive appreciation of quality relating to products and services, but also to management performance and the quality of the organization as a whole in all areas, with the aim of achieving sustained results and long-term success.*

This sentence is unreadable, and it is far too long. Ask yourself what each noun is trying to say, then express that without the noun.

Speedboat Excellence is a program for sustained results and long-term success. It ensures high standards for products and services as well as for management performance and the overall organization.

9. *The capacity for an operator, in one day, for reconditioning plugs, is about 400. (P&R, p. 79)*

An operator can recondition about 400 plugs per day.

10. *To achieve an average failure rate of 500 ppm, corresponding to a 0.05 percent defect probability – i.e. five failures in one million manufactured vehicles – car manufacturers require a defect probability of less than 10 ppm from the system suppliers.*

Simplify this by first putting the text in a sequence of cause → effect. Then, break the text down into several sentences, with only one thought per sentence:

System suppliers must ensure a defect probability of less than 10 ppm. Only then can car manufacturers achieve an average failure rate of 500 ppm. This is equivalent to a 0.05 percent defect probability – i.e. five failures in one million vehicles.

Note: Often, car manufacturers are simply called automakers or carmakers.

11. *The program operates at all levels of the organizational structure: on the one hand through the strong commitment and example of management, on the other through continuous implementation and optimization in teams and the contribution of each individual employee.*

   Remove as many nouns as possible. Note that this "forces" you to write in simple, clear English:

   The program operates at all levels of the organization. Management shows a strong sense of commitment, acting as a role mode. Also, the teams continuously implement and optimize [what? products? processes? You would have to find out]. Each employee contributes to the success of the program.

   This rewriting clarifies who does what, which is important.

12. *The process we use to accomplish these objectives is through the concise description of limitations, the investigation of alternatives, and the establishment of communication channels.* (P&R, p. 79)

   Rewriting this is straightforward, based on the principles applied in the other examples:

   We accomplish these objectives by concisely describing limitations, investigating alternatives, and establishing communication channels.

Chapter 3: Use "...-ing" for complex thoughts

1. *Yachting Excellence is revolutionizing the boating industry and opens up new worlds of experience to spoiled yacht lovers.*

   Rewrite, using the gerund form:

   Yachting Excellence is revolutionizing the boating industry, opening up new worlds of experience to spoiled yacht lovers.

   Note that Yachting Excellence was a quality assurance program of yacht manufacturers.

2. *Check the cable before you check the electrodes.*

   Check the cable before checking the electrodes.

3. *The light sensors are in the shadows, that makes measurement easier.*

   The light sensors are in the shadows, making measurement easier.

4. *Die Umstellung der Bordspannung auf 24 V verursacht weitere Probleme.*

   The background is as follows. Car makers all over the world got together and decided to change the board voltage of automobiles from 12 V to 24 V. The above statement might be an engineers' memo to their boss, informing him that they have been – and still are – encountering difficulties in their efforts to implement the mandated voltage conversion.

   The secret here is to recognize that the sentence contains two statements:

   • Die Bordspannung ist auf 24 V umgestellt worden.
   • Diese Umstellung verursacht weitere Probleme.

   Hence, we can write:

   The board voltage was converted to 24 V, causing additional problems.

   This is an elegant sentence which flows pleasantly. A fundamental principle of technical English is that a sentence should only contain one thought. Hence, we would otherwise have to write **two** sentences:

   The board voltage was converted to 24 V. This is causing additional problems.

   That is choppy and unpleasant to read.

Chapter 4: Avoid the passive voice

1. *Ensure that sufficient storage space is allocated.*

   Allocate sufficient storage space.

   What is "sufficient" storage space? A useful statement is more specific, such as this:
   Allocate 128 bytes of storage space.

2. *Program execution must be halted if measurement errors are discovered.*

   Halt program execution if you discover measurement errors.

3. *Keeping a desired overpressure is accomplished by using a pressure-drop control valve.* (P&R, p. 78)

   Keep a desired overpressure by using a pressure-drop control valve.

   Note that "maintain" is the appropriate verb when referring to a pressure:
   Maintain a desired overpressure by using a pressure-drop control valve.

4. *When the display has been noted and is no longer needed, press the R/S button to proceed with the program.* (P&R, p. 78)

   This sentence is confusing, because it mixes the passive voice with an imperative phrase. The solution is to simply tell the reader what to do:
   When you have noted the information on the display, press the R/S button to proceed with the program.

5. *Ist der Filz verschmutzt, wird er abgezogen und durch einen neuen ersetzt.*

   Assuming the reader is to do something, express this as a command:
   If the felt is dirty, remove it and replace it with a new one.

Chapter 5: Each sentence should communicate only one thought

1. *Unter dem Menüpunkt Kontrolle in der seitlichen Menüleiste können Sie schon erfasste Wand- und Diagonallängen durch eine Kontrollmessung überprüfen.*

   This sentence is making two statements:
   - Die seitliche Menüleiste enthält einen Menüpunkt Kontrolle.
   - Mit diesem Menüpunkt können Sie schon erfasste Wand- und Diagonallängen durch eine Kontrollmessung überprüfen.

   This is easy to express in English:

   The lateral menu bar contains a menu item Check. With this menu item, you can check measured wall and diagonal lengths by means of a test measurement.

2. *Empfehlenswert ist eine Kontrollmessung dann, wenn Sie unsicher sind ob die Messungen mit dem DATA DITTO ordnungsgemäß ausgeführt worden sind, oder nach Abschluss eines Raumes, um sicher zu sein, dass Sie keine Messfehler gemacht haben.*

   Again, break all of this confusing information down into small pieces:

   You should perform a test measurement if you are not sure whether the DATA DITTO conducted the measurements correctly. A test measurement is also a good idea whenever you finish measuring a room, to make sure you did not make any measurement mistakes.

3. *Der gemessene Wert wird im Eingabefeld, der vom Programm errechnete Wert darunter angezeigt.*

   The measured value is displayed in the input field. The value calculated by the program is shown underneath.

4. *The increasing amount of in-boat electronics is causing ever greater complexity in terms of the interactions of individual components and is the biggest challenge facing the boat industry's entire value chain.*

   The increasing amount of in-boat electronics is causing ever greater complexity in terms of the interactions of individual components. This is the biggest challenge facing the boat industry's entire value chain.

5. *The Augsburg is a high-quality press the price is beyond our budget at the present time.*

   The Augsburg is a high-quality press. The price is beyond our budget at the present time.

6. *The TG4 has a stainless steel front this will help in cleaning the oven.*

   The TG4 has a stainless steel front. This will help in cleaning the oven.

Chapter 6: Avoid amputated sentences

1. *Bei Verwendung der Schrittgröße 4 sollte immer dann in das special-Menü zurückgekehrt werden, wenn mit Sicherheit davon auszugehen ist, dass das Ölfilter verschmutzt oder beschädigt ist. Ansonsten Verletzungsgefahr!*

   Attempts to translate "Ansonsten Verletzungsgefahr" in this compact form will simply not work. Expressions such as "Else injury hazard", "Else danger of injuries" sound very odd. I recommend expressing Ansonsten Verletzungsgefahr as a fully written-out sentence. This is one solution:

   Otherwise, you might injure yourself!

2. *Auswahl der Leerfahrfunktion generell nur bei vorherIger Entfernung aller Flaschen vom Förderband möglich! Sonst Flaschenstau!*

   Expressions such as "Else bottle jam" are poor English, because we simply do not express such things this way. I suggest, for example:

   Else, the bottles will back up.

   Note that "the bottles back up" means that they cannot continue moving forward (Germans would speak of "Stau" or "Rückstau"). The statement "the bottles jam" is slightly different. This means that bottles are stuck in place and (typically) cannot be removed - as from a dispensing machine (in German, "Die Flaschen klemmen").

3. *Die Voraussetzung für die Benutzung der Maus ist jedoch die Auswahl des Treibers L1 durch den autorisierten Benutzer (Punkt Maustreiber im Menü Systemeinstellungen). Bei Verwendung des falschen Treibers bzw. Nichtauswahl eines Treibers erfolgt Fehl-funktion der Maus. Nach Auswahl des Treibers Warmstart des Rechners erforderlich (Reset).*

   Fully write out the information in the parentheses:

   [...] the authorized user. For this, select the menu item Mouse Driver in the menu System Settings. [...] After you have selected the driver, re-start the computer by pressing the Reset button.

   Notice that I have removed the parentheses. The information in them has now become part of the body text, so these punctuation marks are un-necessary. They would only distract the reader.

4. *Rückspulen des Bandes durch gleichzeitiges Drücken der Tasten Back und Tape. Hörbares Bandendegeräusch nach Erreichen des Bandendes dann Stop drücken.*

   Rewind the tape by pressing the buttons Back and Tape simultaneous-ly. You will hear a noise when the recorder reaches the end of the tape. Then press the Stop button.

5. *Verlassen dieses Eingabefensters nur nach Anwahl der einzelnen Optionen möglich (oder Cancel drücken).*

   Before exiting this input window, you must select an option or press Cancel.

6. *Der Filename wird nach Drücken von Return in der Titelleiste bestätigt.*

   When you press Return, the file name will be shown in the title bar.

7. *Es wird nur jeder zweite Anschluss aktiviert (trotz Unterschreitens der Höchstteilnehmerzahl).*

   Only every other connection is enabled (although the ??? has dropped below the maximum number of subscribers).

   The question marks above indicate that information is missing: What has decreased?

8. *Im Eingabefenster wird das Passwort generell zweimal eingegeben.*

   In the input window, always enter your password twice.

9. *Bestätigen der Eingabe mit Return.*

   Confirm your entry by pressing Return.

10. *Nach Erreichen des Sollwertes wird die Anlage abgeschaltet.*

    The system will be switched off when the desired value is reached.

Chapter 7: Decompress compact wordings

1. *Please take note of the reduced grease utilization period of the ball bearings after storage periods exceeding one year.*

   Find out what the author is trying to say, and write that. An example might be something like this:

   If the ball bearings are stored for more than one year, the grease will dry out. Thus, you must …

   The author actually wants someone to **do** something. Find out what that is, and tell your reader to do it. The original sentence ("Please take note of the reduced grease utilization period …") is poor writing, because it does not tell the reader what to do.

2. *Die Transistoren T14 und T9 sehen ähnlich aus, Vertauschungsgefahr!*

   Transistors T14 and T9 look about the same. Do not confuse the one with the other.

3. *Save the data if necessary.*

   This does not tell the reader when saving the data might be necessary, so the sentence is essentially useless. Find out when the data must be saved, and say that. Here is an example:

   If the space available on your hard disk drive drops below 53 MB, then save the data.

   Depending on how much experience your readers have, you might need to tell them how to determine the available hard disk space.

4. *Wasserstand kontrollieren, evtl. nachfüllen.*

   Tell the reader exactly what to do. Here is an example:

   Check the water level. Add water if the level is less than 5 cm.

5. *The motor must be dried if the insulation resistance is not adequate.*

   Obtain the missing information, and restate this as specifically as possible, such as:

   Dry the motor if the insulation resistance is less than 17 MΩ.

Chapter 8: First word = conceptual subject

1. *The responsibility for overriding blood pressure monitoring lies with the physician.*

   What is this statement mostly about? A native speaker of English would probably consider the physician to be most important:

   The physician is responsible for overriding blood pressure monitoring.

   The author's intention is probably more like this:

   Only a physician is allowed to override blood pressure monitoring.

2. *Die Befehle werden jeden Samstag ausgeführt.*

   These commands are executed every Saturday.

3. *Die Namen der Maschinen werden jetzt im Eingabefenster eingegeben.*

   Is this something the reader is supposed to do? If so, write:

   Enter the names of the machines in the input window.

   If this is general information (e.g., part of a system description):

   The names of the machines are now entered in the input window.

4. *Click in the main window on the Align tab.*

   In the main window, click on the Align tab.

   The important thing is to keep the main message together. Note that this word order – with "In the main window …" first – harmonizes well with what the reader is probably focusing on. He or she first goes to the main window, and then finds the Align tab.

5. *Data between two computers is transmitted by modems.*
   (P&R, p. 74)

   Depending on what is important:
   * *Modems transmit data between two computers.*
   * *Two computers send and receive data via modems.*
   * *Data between two computers is transmitted by modems.*

6. *In service mode, the status of the inlets and outlets can be checked.*

   If the aspect of service mode is unimportant, write:
   The status of the inlets and outlets can be checked in service mode.

   If service mode is to be emphasized, then the sentence can be left unchanged.

   Or simplify by adding a subheading:
   In service mode
   Check the status of the inlets and outlets.

   Or:
   In service mode
   The status of the inlets and outlets can be checked.

7. *After the fault is eliminated, a reference run must be made.*

   I would tend to leave the sentence the way it is. The word order complies with the sequence: cause → effect, which is helpful here.

8. *Vor Eingabe der benötigten Zahlen liest der Benutzer die Anweisung durch.*

   As part of a user manual:
   Read the instructions before you enter the required numbers.

   Or:
   Read the instructions. Then enter the required numbers.

   Or:
   1. Read the instructions.
   2. Enter the required numbers.

   As part of a system description:
   The user reads the instructions before entering the required numbers.

Chapter 9: Do not overwrite

1. *In dem Feld Dateinamen wird der programmintern angelegte Dateiname für den jeweiligen Gebäudeabschnitt zur Information angezeigt.*

   Decide which words are conveying important information and which ones are not really saying anything. Ignore the latter. Express the important information as simply as possible:
   The field File Name displays the program's file name for each building section.

2. *In caring for your mixer, you should remember to care for it like you would any other electrical appliance.* (P&R, p. 82)

   Care for your mixer like you would any other electrical appliance.

3. *The plate is supported again by a thick wire that extends down into a connecting pin in the base, and the exact position of the pin is the pin next to the notch in the base.* (P&R, p. 82)

   The plate is supported by a thick wire extending down into a base pin, located next to the notch in the base.

Chapter 11: Address your readers directly

1. *Nun wird der Lautsprecher montiert, dazu soll als erstes die An-schlusslitzen 48 und 49 auf die richtige Länge von jeweils 60 mm gebracht werden.*

   Mount the speaker. For this, cut speaker wires 48 and 49 to a length of 60 mm.

   Or use a subheading:
   Mounting the speaker
   Cut speaker wires 48 and 49 to a length of 60 mm.

2. *Jetzt wird die andere Schutzfolie abgezogen und nun kann der Lautsprecher auf die Leiterplatte geklebt werden.*

   Remove the other protective film. Glue the speaker onto the PCB.

3. *Compliance with the safety precautions of Chapter 2 is necessary.*

   Comply with the safety precautions of Chapter 2.

   Note, however, that this is not very specific. What exactly is the reader supposed to do?

4. *Seals must be glued in on one side.*

   Glue the seals in on one side.

Chapter 12: Be careful with noun-verb combinations

Vor der jeweiligen Geräte-Gleichstrom-Speisungseinheit findet eine Wandlung vom zugeführten Versorgungsnetz mit Wechselspannung (110 V / 60 Hz oder 230 V / 50 Hz) statt.

The line voltage is converted from AC (110 V at 60 Hz or 230 V at 50 Hz) to DC, before it is applied to the power connection for each device.

The stylistic trap here is to say something like "... a conversion takes place ...". That would be very stilted writing, and your readers might not understand you.

Chapter 13: Unfold your sentences

1. *Die in einer Reihe von internationalen Studien vielfach belegte Wirksamkeit des Mittels ist durch die Untersuchungen von Prof. Schneider – noch einmal – zweifelsfrei bewiesen worden.*

   Note that this sentence contains two statements:
   - Eine Reihe von internationalen Studien hat die Wirksamkeit des Mittels vielfach belegt.
   - Die Untersuchungen von Prof. Schneider haben diese Wirksamkeit noch einmal zweifelsfrei bewiesen.

   Clearly separating the two statements makes it easy to translate them:
   Numerous international studies have repeatedly demonstrated the effectiveness of the medicine. The investigations of Prof. Schneider underscore again how potent it is.

2. *Dabei war nicht vorgegeben, jedoch erwünscht, mit einer relativ großen Versuchspersonenanzahl Aussagen in Richtung möglichst "hoher, statistischer Signifikanz" zu treffen.*

   It was desired (but not stipulated) that a relatively large number of test persons would make statements of considerable statistical significance.

Chapter 14: Use simple verbs

1. *Based on the Total Quality Management system, Speedboat Excellence constitutes an integrated approach for efficiently ensuring the quality of products and services with a zero-defect objective consonant with customer requirements in the speedboat industry.*

   Speedboat Excellence is an integrated approach, based on the Total Quality Management system. It efficiently ensures high-quality products and services. The goal – zero defects – is what speedboat customers require.

   Or:

   Based on the Total Quality Management system, Speedboat Excellence is an integrated approach ensuring high-quality products and services. The goal – zero defects – is what speedboat customers require.

2. *The sensors are located in the tank.*

   The sensors are in the tank.

3. *Erst nach Vorliegen eines ausreichenden Behälter-Füllstandes kann mit der Flaschenreinigung begonnen werden.*

   What is ausreichender Behälter-Füllstand? Does the author mean: When the container is full? Then, we can write:
   Clean the bottles only when the container is full.

   Walt Disney, a master of communication and crowd management, would probably ask:
   Is the container full? Then clean the bottles.

   If the container does not need to be full, but rather some specific minimum level of a liquid is required, then we must specify that level. An example would be:
   Clean the bottles only when the level of [water ...] in the container is 5 cm or more.

   Of course, if the operator does nothing and a machine cleans the bottles, then we write:
   The bottles can only be cleaned when the container is full (when the level in the container is 5 cm or more).

Chapter 16: Express concrete ideas in a concrete way, especially if people are involved

1. *Der Vorschlag ist gekommen ...*

   Find out who is making the suggestion. Then make a specific statement, such as:

   John Nielson suggested ...

2. *Dies ist – vermutlich! – eine Aufforderung zum Handeln.*

   They are probably trying to tell people to do something.

   It would be a good idea to find out who is involved and who is supposed to act.

3. *"'Es gibt keine grundlegende Abkehr von diesem Kurs', erklärten ihre Sprecher Andrea Nahles und Michael Müller in Berlin" (Süddeutsche Zeitung for May 26, 2005)*

   Compared to German, English is direct and concrete. Technical English is even more so. Regarding the above quotation, we would talk about people and what is happening in their minds:

   Nobody is talking about fundamentally changing course.

Chapter 17: Your sentences should flow

1. *Sie können die Ausmaße von Türen ändern (Breite ändern, Höhe ändern) oder die Lage in einer Wand neu bestimmen (horizontal bzw. vertikal verschieben).*

   The secret here: Do not try to put all of the information in a single sentence.

   You can redefine a door's dimensions or position in a wall.

   Redefining a door's dimensions
   You can change the width or height of the door.

   Redefining a door's position in a wall
   You can move the door horizontally or vertically.

2. *Bei Anwendung eines 5-Ω drahtgewickelten (Präzisions-) bzw. eines 75-Ω NTC-Widerstands (Baureihe RW 450 bzw. 324) bzw. bei Einsatz in rauer Umgebung …*

   This can be stated neatly by using a structure:

   … when using:
   a 5-Ω wire-wound precision resistor, or
   a 75-Ω NTC resistor (series RW 450 or 324), or
   […?] in harsh environments

3. *The computer is a Model 1. It is 7 years old. It does not have sufficient RAM. No new programs will run on it.*

   The computer, a Model 1, is seven years old. It does not have very much RAM, so no new programs will run on it.

4. *The taste test is important in food development. The test is run by lab technicians. The technicians are supervised by a sensory evaluator. (P&R, p. 82)*

   The taste test is important in food development. It is run by lab technicians supervised by a sensory evaluator.

Chapter 18: Use commas properly

1. *This section shows a template to store a routing tree to the ABC database by using the XYZ batch interface.*

   This section shows a template to store a routing tree to the ABC database, using the XYZ batch interface.

2. *The thresholds must be combined making sure that only one threshold can be reached at a certain time.*

   The thresholds must be combined, making sure that only one threshold can be reached at a certain time.

3. *He claimed, the best essay was submitted by your sister.*

   He claimed the best essay was submitted by your sister.

4. *For a description of the monitor settings see section 5.8.7 "Rate Plan for the Discount feature".*

   For a description of the monitor settings, see section 5.8.7 "Rate Plan for the Discount feature".

5. *Three accumulators count the administrator's CPU usage as follows.*

   Three accumulators count the administrator's CPU usage, as follows.

6. *In my opinion the publishing date should be moved up but I realize this may cause hardship for some people.*

   In my opinion, the publishing date should be moved up. However, I realize this may cause hardship for some people.

7. *She said, the work must be done whether you like it or not.*

   She said the work must be done – whether you like it or not.

8. *Paul Jones the owner of a large luxurious sophisticated yacht a classic Fedship from the Netherlands arrived at the port on time.*

   Paul Jones, the owner of a large, luxurious, sophisticated yacht (a classic Fedship from the Netherlands) arrived at the port on time.

9. *This section provides a functional description of the Discount feature and shows the corresponding service data.*

   This section provides a functional description of the Discount feature, and shows the corresponding service data.

   Or:

   This section provides a functional description of the Discount feature, showing the corresponding service data.

10. *For the SuperMFJ feature the same conditions apply as for the ARkE feature (see above).*

    For the SuperMFJ feature, the same conditions apply as for the ARkE feature (see above).

Chapter 19: Use hyphens properly

1. *The problem, however, cannot be solved as described in the e-mail-message.*

   The problem, however, cannot be solved as described in the e-mail message.

2. *The user's name must be entered in the Name-Field.*

   Write Name (with an initial capital letter) if Name Field is a proper noun. This is the case, for example, if the user interface uses this exact designation for the field. If this concept is not a proper noun, then name field is correct.

   The user's name must be entered in the name field.

   Or:

   The user's name must be entered in the Name field.

3. *In my opinion, the printing-date should be pushed back. However,*
    this could cause hardship for some people.

    In my opinion, the printing date should be pushed back. However, this
    could cause hardship for some people.

4. *Depending on the noise level, the customer must take all required*
    steps to protect operating personnel in accordance with noise
    protection regulations and standards.

    Depending on the noise level, the customer must take all required
    steps to protect operating personnel. This must be done in accordance
    with noise-protection regulations and standards.

5. *The PC-cable is broken.*

    The PC cable is broken.

6. *The radio needs new 1½ volt batteries, I believe.*

    The radio needs new 1½-volt batteries, I believe.

7. *The 4-liter-hat is too big for my head.*

    The 4-liter hat is too big for my head.

8. *I talk on my handy all the time since I have this flat-rate.*

    "Flat rate" is correct for British English – but without the hyphen! Speak-
    ers of American English would use the term unlimited plan; more precise-
    ly unlimited call plan or unlimited pay plan.
    I use my cellphone all the time, now that I have an unlimited pay plan.
    (American English)

    Or:
    I use my mobile phone all the time, now that I have a flat rate.
    (British English)

Wrap-up exercises

A. Improve the following sentences

1. *We must inform each employee that she must fill out a W-4-form. (P&R, p. 83)*

   We must tell the employees to fill out a W-4 form.

2. *There are five basic requirements that a software must fulfill.*

   Software must fulfill five basic requirements.

3. *It is maintained by the user that ...*

   The user maintains that ...

4. *The user must fill in the required informations in the field Mask-name.*

   In English, the word information is often implicitly plural, without a final s. There is no English word informations. The user must fill in the information required in the field Mask Name.

5. *It is believed that ...*

   Mr. Jones believes that ...

6. *Your complaint has been received by our company, and ...*

   Our company has received your complaint, and ...

7. *By entering a two-digit parameter, the time is selected.*

   Select the time by entering a two-digit parameter.

8. *After the time "dup2" runs out, the connection to the remote-station is built up.*

   After the time "dup2" expires, the connection to the remote station is established.

B. Translate the following sentences into English

1. *Nach erfolgter Prüfung seiner Login-Kennung übernimmt der Benutzer Administratoraufgaben.*

   After his or her user name and password have been checked, the user can perform administrative tasks.

2. *Die Überprüfung der in das OMC noch nicht übertragenen Datenbits erfordert einen zweiten Eintrag in das Heimatregister.*

   A second entry must be made in the Home register, before the bits which have not yet been transferred to the OMC can be checked.

   Or use a subheading:
   Checking the bits not yet transferred to the OMC
   A second entry in the Home register is required.

3. *Das bereits vorher eingegebene Beispiel soll in der Datei "Field lengths" abgespeichert werden.*

   Store the entered example in the file "Field lengths".

4. *Der neue Mikroprozessor-Chip ist in 0,25-µm-Technik realisiert.*

   The new microprocessor chip is implemented in 0.25-µm technology.

5. *Die Schnittstelle ist im vorliegenden Gerät als leistungsfähiges 320-bps-Ausgabeport realisiert.*

   The interface in this device is a powerful 320-bps output port.

6. *Die Rechte eines Administrators erhält der Benutzer erst nach Prüfung seiner Login-Kennung.*

   The user has administrative privileges only after his or her user name and password have been checked.

7. *„,Es gibt keine grundlegende Abkehr von diesem Kurs', erklärten ihre Sprecher Andrea Nahles und Michael Müller in Berlin".*
   (Süddeutsche Zeitung for May 26, 2005)

   Nobody is talking about fundamentally changing course.

8. *Es findet ein Umdenken statt.*

   People are changing how they think about …

Literature

Pauley, Steven E. and Daniel G. Riordan (1993[5]). Technical report writing today. Boston: Houghton Mifflin.

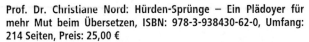

Prof. Dr. Christiane Nord: Hürden-Sprünge – Ein Plädoyer für mehr Mut beim Übersetzen, ISBN: 978-3-938430-62-0, Umfang: 214 Seiten, Preis: 25,00 €

Anhand von 100 Beispielen mit Übersetzungen in deutscher, englischer, französischer, spanischer, italienischer, portugiesischer, chinesischer, arabischer, türkischer, russischer, dänischer, schwedischer Sprache und in Afrikaans zeigt die Autorin, was es bedeutet, beim Übersetzen nicht nur Texte in anderen Sprachen zu produzieren, sondern Texte, die auch über die „kulturelle Hürde" kommen. Dabei geht es um folgende Textsorten: Garantiezertifikate, Stellenangebote, Presseberichte, Handelskorrespondenz, Nachrichten, medizinische Packungsbeilagen, Wartungs- und Gebrauchsanleitungen, Autoatlanten, Lehr-, Fach-, Sach- und Kinderbücher, Autobiografien, Essays, Romane, Erzählungen, Märchen, Krimis, Theaterstücke, Gedichte, Kinderlieder, politische Songs, Comics, Schilder im öffentlichen Raum, eine (mündliche) Stadtführung in Hanoi und das Neue Testament. Zahlreiche „Mutproben" (zu denen es auch entsprechende Hilfestellungen gibt) helfen den Leserinnen und Lesern, selbst auszuprobieren, ob sie schon genügend Mut für einen eleganten Hürden-Sprung erworben haben.

Renate Dockhorn: SDL Trados Studio 2014 für Einsteiger und Umsteiger – Bild-zu-Bild-Anleitung, ISBN: 978-3-938430-57-6, Umfang: 337 Seiten, Preis: 29,00 €

SDL Trados Studio 2014 gehört zu den Marktführern unter den Translation-Memory-Systemen, die aus vielen Bereichen der Übersetzungstätigkeit inzwischen nicht mehr wegzudenken sind. Ob der Nutzer dieses Werkzeug effektiv und effizient nutzen kann, hängt maßgeblich davon ab, wie gut sie oder er diese komplexen Werkzeuge beherrscht. Das gilt vor allem für alle Neulinge – egal ob man das erste Mal mit einem TM-System arbeitet oder erstmals mit SDL Trados Studio 2014. Das Buch eignet sich für die selbständige Einarbeitung in die Software, als Begleitmaterial für Schulungen und auch für die Nachbereitung von Schulungen und ist ein ideales Nachschlagewerk, das auf keinem Schreibtisch fehlen sollte.

Die Autorin hat mit dieser Einführung in Studio 2014 und das zugehörige Terminologieverwaltungsprogramm SDL Multiterm 2014 eine systematischen Schritt-für-Schritt-Anleitung verfasst, die der ideale Begleiter beim erfolgreichen Einstieg in oder Umstieg auf dieses Tool ist. In Hunderten von farbigen Screenshots führt sie den Nutzer durch die verschiedenen Menüs vom Erstmaligen Einrichten über die verschiedenen Ansichten, das Arbeiten mit Projekten, Paketen und Einzeldateien bis hin zu AutoSuggest, Qualitätssicherung und Überprüfung.

Alle Preise sind Bruttopreise und verstehen sich zzgl. Porto und Verpackung (ab 2,50 €). Bestellungen erbitten wir bevorzugt über unsere Internetseite: www.fachverlag.bdue.de. Dort finden Sie außerdem Leseproben zum kostenlosen Download.